# The Loving Energy of Reiki

Join me in a magical mission by leaving a review on Amazon for my Reiki kids book, and together we can empower young minds with the enchanting power of words.

Namaste, Miriam

★★★★★

Copyright © 2023 by Miriam Bueno
Artwork by Miriam Bueno
All rights reserved. www.connectiongoal.com
First printing, 2023

Hello, little one!
This is a book all about Reiki, a loving energy that surrounds us.

Let's discover the wonders of Reiki together!

Reiki starts with love in our hearts.
Can you feel your heart beating?
It's full of love just for you!

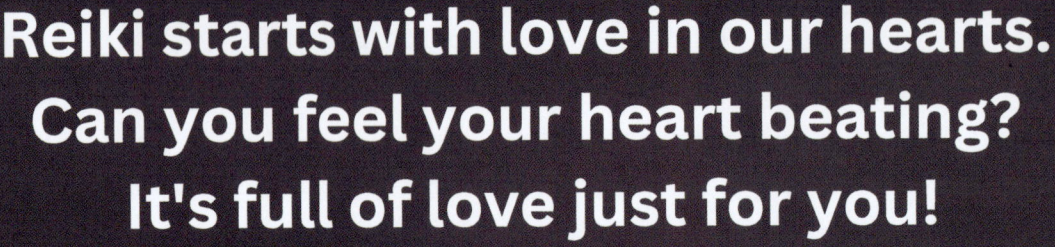

It's full of love just for you!

Reiki is like a warm hug.
It's a gentle touch that makes you feel safe and calm.

Did you know that you can share Reiki with your toys?

Touch them gently and send them love and comfort.

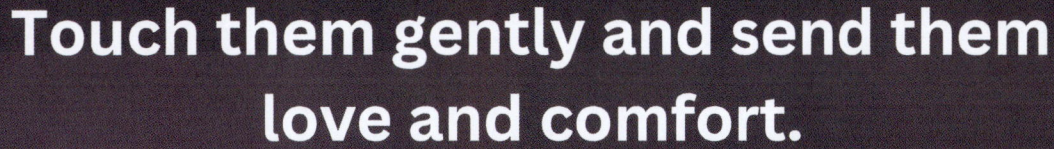

Pets love Reiki too!
When you stroke them gently,
you're sharing the loving energy of
Reiki with them.

Reiki is all around us, even in nature. When you feel the soft grass or listen to the rustling leaves, you're connecting with the healing energy of Reiki.

You can also give Reiki to yourself. Place your hands on your tummy and take deep breaths.

Feel the love and peace flowing through you.

Close your eyes and imagine soft, sparkling light surrounding you. It's like a cozy blanket of love.

# Reiki can help calm your mind.

Gently place your hands on your head and imagine worries floating away, leaving space for happiness and peace.

With Reiki, we can share love and kindness with everyone we meet.

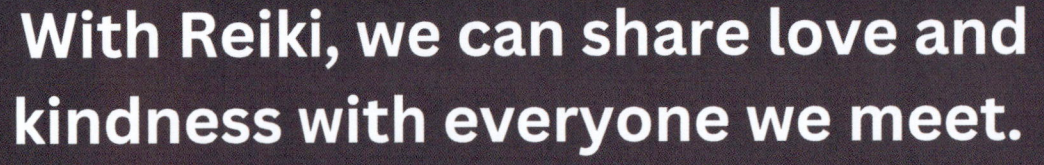

Let's spread joy and make the world a brighter place!

Thank you for joining our Reiki adventure! Remember, you are surrounded by love and the healing energy of Reiki.

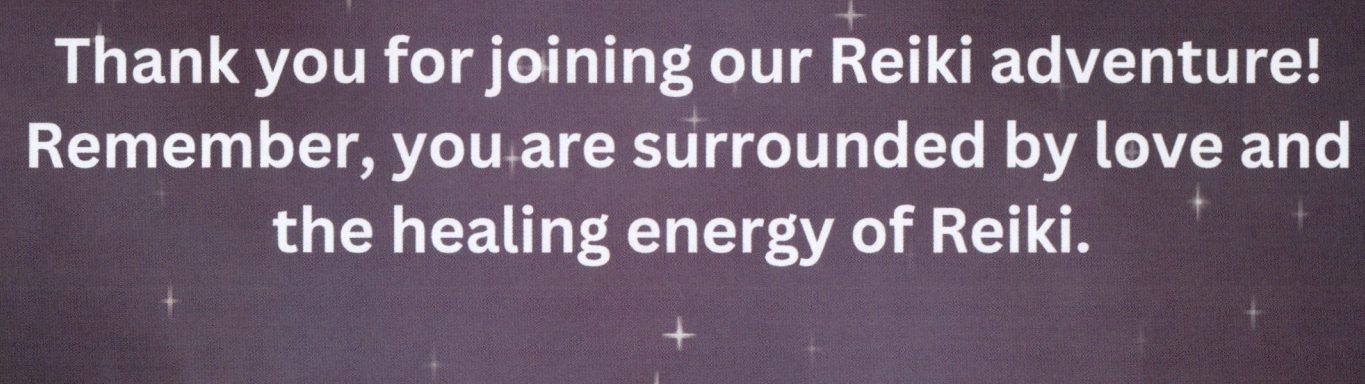

Embrace it, share it, and let your heart shine brightly, little one.

Printed in Great Britain
by Amazon